Lives and Times

Louis Braille

Jayne Woodhouse

Heinemann
LIBRARY

www.heinemann.co.uk
Visit our website to find out more information about Heinemann Library books.

To order:

 Phone 44 (0) 1865 888066

 Send a fax to 44 (0) 1865 314091

 Visit the Heinemann Bookshop at www.heinemann.co.uk to browse our catalogue and order online.

First published in Great Britain by Heinemann Library
Halley Court, Jordan Hill, Oxford OX2 8EJ,
a division of Reed Educational and Professional Publishing Ltd.
Heinemann is a registered trademark of Reed Educational and Professional Publishing Ltd.

OXFORD FLORENCE PRAGUE MADRID ATHENS
MELBOURNE AUCKLAND KUALA LUMPUR SINGAPORE TOKYO
IBADAN NAIROBI KAMPALA JOHANNESBURG GABORONE
PORTSMOUTH NH (USA) CHICAGO MEXICO CITY SAO PAULO

Designed by Ken Vail Graphic Design, Cambridge
Illustrated by Hemesh Alles
Originated by Dot Gradations Ltd
Printed and bound by South China Printing in Hong Kong/China

ISBN 0 431 13453 7 (hardback)   ISBN 0 431 13458 8 (paperback)
06 05 04 03 02   06 05 04 03 02
10 9 8 7 6 5 4 3 2 1   10 9 8 7 6 5 4 3 2 1

British Library Cataloguing in Publication Data

Woodhouse, Jayne
Louis Braille. – (Lives and times) (Take-off!)
1. Braille, Louis, 1805–1852 – Juvenile literature
2. Educators – France – Biography – Juvenile literature
3. Braille – History – Juvenile literature
I. Title
362.4'1'092

Acknowledgements
The publishers would like to thank the following for permission to reproduce photographs:
Eye Ubiquitous/Paul Seheult, pp. 17, 18, 19, 20, 21, 22, 23.

Cover photograph: Mary Evans Picture Library.

Our thanks to Betty Root for her comments in the preparation of this book.

Every effort has been made to contact copyright holders of any material reproduced in this book.
Any omissions will be rectified in subsequent printings if notice is given to the publishers.

Contents

What is braille?.. 4

Childhood 6

A terrible accident 8

Going to school 10

A wonderful idea 12

Developing braille....................................14

Louis dies...16

Portraits and artefacts 18

Museums and artefacts 20

Buildings..22

Glossary.. 24

Index 24

Any words appearing in the text in bold,
like this, are explained in the Glossary.

What is braille?

Do you know how blind people read? They use books written in **braille**. The books have little raised dots instead of letters.

These children are reading with their fingers, not their eyes.

raised dots

fingers

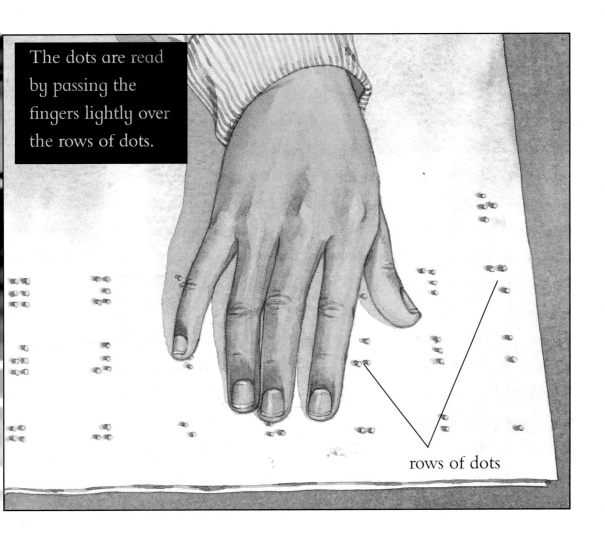

The dots are read by passing the fingers lightly over the rows of dots.

rows of dots

Braille is named after **Louis Braille**, the man who invented this special writing for blind people. This is his story.

Childhood

Louis Braille was born in France in 1809, nearly 200 years ago. His father was a **saddler**.

Louis Braille was born on 4 January 1809 near Paris, France.

Louis's father

sharp tool

leather harness

When he was a little boy, Louis loved to play in his father's workshop. 'Don't touch the knives!' said his father. 'They are too sharp for you.'

Louis liked to be with his father in the workshop.

Louis

workbench

A terrible accident

One day, when he was three, Louis picked up a knife. He tried to cut with it. But the knife slipped and went into his eye.

Louis damaged his eye with one of his father's knives.

father

mother

Louis

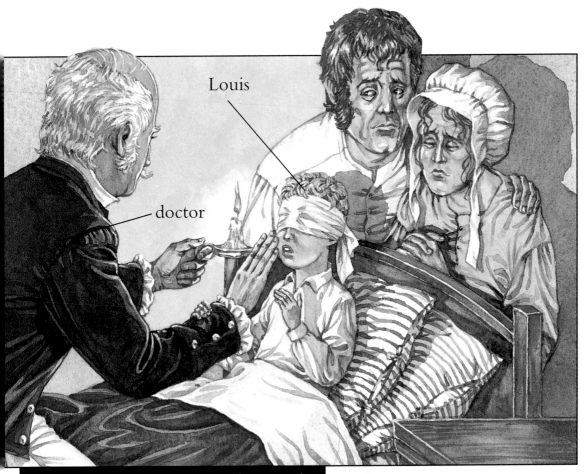

Louis

doctor

Both of Louis's eyes were damaged.

Then his other eye began to hurt too. The doctor could not help. Soon Louis could not see. He was blind.

Going to school

When Louis was ten, he went to a special school for blind children. It was in **Paris**, a long way away from his home.

Louis

Louis had to go to this special school for blind children.

Before **braille** was invented, blind people had to read by touching large letters made of wood, cardboard or lead.

large letters

big books

It was slow and hard to read letters that stood out.

Louis learnt to read with great big books. The letters stood out. He had to feel each letter with his fingers.

A wonderful idea

Louis wanted to find a quicker way to read. When he was only 13, he had a clever idea. 'I will change the letters into dots,' he said. 'Then they will be easier to feel.'

Louis decided to change the letters into dots.

dots

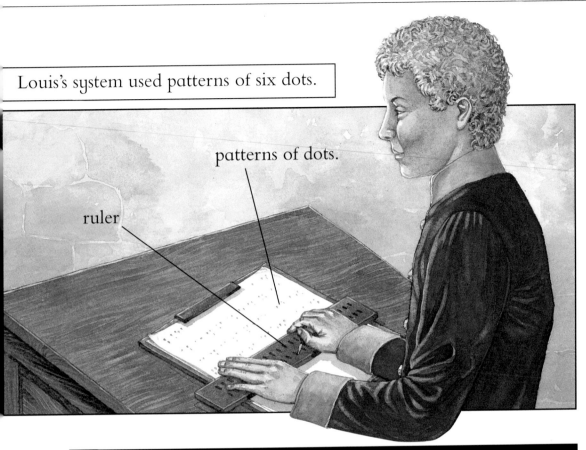

Louis's system used patterns of six dots.

patterns of dots.

ruler

Using patterns of dots made reading and writing much easier.

Louis made up a pattern of dots for each letter. He made a special ruler to press the dots into the paper. The dots stuck out so you could feel them.

Developing braille

The teachers did not like Louis's idea. 'You cannot use this here!' they said.

Louis

teachers

The teachers did not want to use this new system.

Louis became a teacher at the School for Blind Youth in 1826.

pupil

Louis

Louis was an excellent teacher.

When Louis grew up, he became a teacher at the school. He never forgot his idea. He made it better and better.

Louis dies

Louis was very sad that no one liked his idea for making reading and writing for blind people easier. He became very ill.

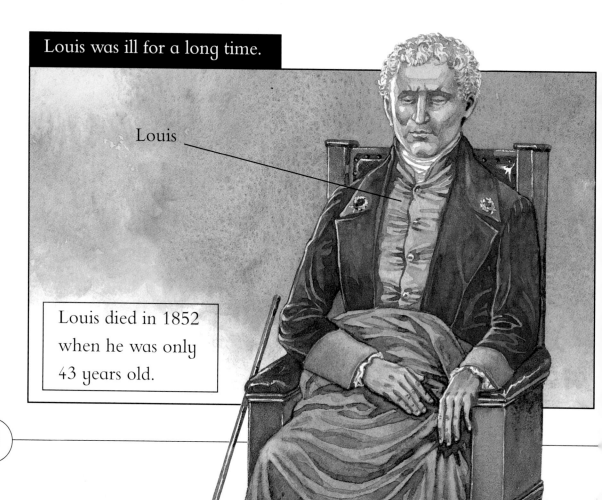

Louis was ill for a long time.

Louis

Louis died in 1852 when he was only 43 years old.

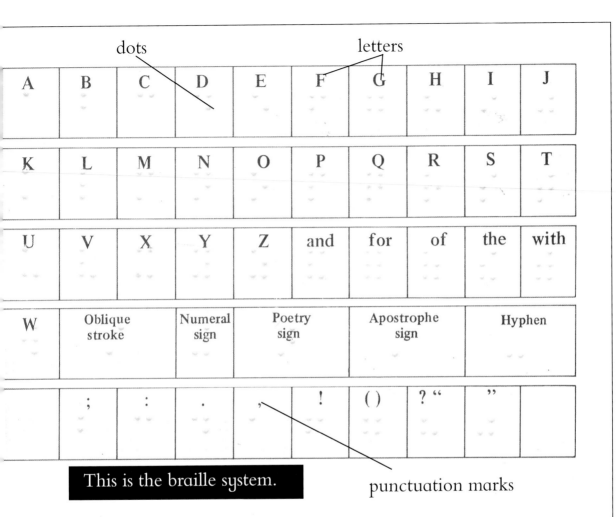

dots   letters

A	B	C	D	E	F	G	H	I	J
K	L	M	N	O	P	Q	R	S	T
U	V	X	Y	Z	and	for	of	the	with
W	Oblique stroke	Numeral sign	Poetry sign		Apostrophe sign		Hyphen		
	;	:	.	,	!	( )	? "	"	

This is the braille system.

punctuation marks

Not long after his death, people saw that Louis's dots really were a good idea. Today blind people all over the world use **braille** to read and write.

Louis even devised a braille system for reading and writing music!

Portraits and artefacts

This is a **portrait** of **Louis Braille**.

It shows you what he looked like.

Louis Braille's portrait

The School for Blind Youth started using the braille system in 1854, two years after Louis's death.

Louis's dominoes

Louis liked to play with dominoes.

These are some dominoes that Louis played with. You can see them in the house where Louis was born.

Have you ever played with dominoes? Why do you think Louis liked to play with them?

Museums and artefacts

You can still see the house where Louis was born.
It is now a **museum**. Inside, you can see some of
his family's belongings,
like his dominoes.

Do you
remember
when he
was born?
Read page 6
again to see
if you were
right!

house

Louis was
born in this
house.

This is the workshop where Louis's father worked. It was here, with one of these tools, that Louis hurt his eye.

Look at all the sharp tools.

Buildings

This is a photograph of Louis's special school.

The **braille** system has 63 dot patterns. It can be hard for blind people to learn it.

The special school for the blind which Louis went to is still there in **Paris**.

Louis Braille was buried in this tomb.

tomb

If you ever go to Paris, you can visit the **tomb** where **Louis Braille** is buried. It is in a famous building called the **Panthéon**.

Glossary

This glossary explains difficult words, and tells you how to say words which are hard to say.

artefacts   things which people make and use, like tools, clothes and cooking pots. We can learn about the past by looking at old artefacts. You say *arty-facts*.

braille   raised dots on paper which blind people use to read and write. You say *breyl*.

Louis Braille   You say *loo-ee breyl*. (French people say *bry*.)

museum   building that has lots of artefacts in it which tell us about the past

Panthéon   a building in Paris where you can see the tombs of many famous people. You say *pan-they-on*.

Paris   the capital city of France

portrait   picture of a person, showing their face

saddler   person who makes and repairs saddles and leather harnesses for horses

tomb   where a dead person is buried

Index

becomes blind 9
birth 6, 20
braille 4, 5, 14, 17, 23
death 16
France 6

knife 7, 8
museum 20, 21
new way of reading 12
Paris 10, 22

portrait 18
special school 10, 15, 22
teaching 15
tomb 23